NASHE - WITH GOD – The Journey of a Transformed Woman

Tinashe Mujera

Published by NaShe Nhasi, 2024.

NASHE - WITH GOD – THE JOURNEY OF A TRANSFORMED WOMAN

First edition. April 17, 2024.

Copyright © 2024 Tinashe Mujera.

ISBN: 979-8224196357

Written by Tinashe Mujera.

To my beautiful daughter Atarah, you inspire me always to be all that God has called me to be. To my late parents, thank you.

To every woman and man who will read this book, may you find your true self!

NASHE

- WITH GOD –

The Journey of a Transformed Woman
TINASHE MUJERA

Layout design by Boutique Books
Cover design by Mark on Africa Digital
Printed in South Africa by Digital Action

Dedication

To my beautiful daughter Atarah, you inspire me always to be all that God has called me to be. To my late parents, thank you.
To every woman and man who will read this book, may you find your true self!
Nashe -With God- The journey of a Transformed woman

Reviews

A heart gripping true story, full of translation; from an excruciating experience of emotional struggles and inner defiant pain, to the eventual embrace of, and submission to the unwavering depth of the pure embrace that God's Love provides for his children. An absolute must read!

- Dipo Adeda- Osinloye

This is a story of survival. Each time your faith is tested, you have to keep digging even deeper for strength and determination. Definitely the story of a female Job. You get to understand how some losses and obstacles build character. "Be soft, be the flower, but the powerful force underneath"

Furthermore, sometimes our daily existence or so called "luck" relies on the kindness of strangers. This book is a clear testimony of such

- Dali Nolasco- (Bradley Dali)

Nashe -With God- The journey of a Transformed woman

Epigraph

"Owning our story and loving ourselves through that process is the bravest thing that we will ever do."

- Brene' Brown

Preface

Tinashe has invested time in the presence of the Lord to carefully capture not only the story but also the courageous spirit of a slave girl who becomes a queen.

The author compared and paralleled her life with Esther as a profound prophetic template in shaping this excellent work, written for the benefit and development of the Body of Christ, especially teenage girls, who will one day become spiritually sound women and mothers in their various works of life.

The use of Esther as an image reality of femininity on a journey of becoming... and how God defines and uses his invested prophetic seed and plans in his children to shape what each of them is designed for is an excellent and powerful valued concept highlighted.

Undoubtedly, every woman, regardless of their past conditions, is wired to shape, influence, and transform her world. This book will continue to captivate your mind as it reveals the dynamic nature of the Father, as he recaptures his image and likeness in the life of an apprehended woman for his glory.

As you may know, womanhood is a calling, mission, and prophetic voice in representing the Lord's eternal intentions for humanity. This book has revealed some of the most profound ways, patterns, and processes of God's dealings, and highlights the priceless value of a woman called a voice of hope, courage, and visionary leadership strength in a time of great distress and perplexity as we see today.

There are quite a few books that I have read with the desire to challenge other women to find their purpose and achieve greatness for themselves. What many of these well-written books lack, however, is one: God's unique divine blueprint for each woman and the corporate spirit of womanhood as biblically prescribed.

Secondly, the courage of authenticity to confront who they are, and then allow God to use the misfortunes, pain, fear, doubt, and insecurity of their lives as a template that sets out the path to engage God's inherent word until the process of healing, transformation, and restoration becomes manifest.

The reality is that each of us is a mirror, a reflection of inner struggles often sowed as a seed, while trying to find our own self-identity as a teenager in a world plagued by complex dysfunctional socio-cultural realities.

This material is an excellent resource in terms of the guide to identifying the true image of a woman beyond the way a blind, post-truth culture has defined or is currently shaping her. The inspiration I perceive in this book could be similar to the image of a woman in a puzzle piece, which is searched and arranged since each part of her image is located to fit into their ordained positions.

This is a book that reflects what the Lord is doing, not only in the life of the author but also in the lives of all women in search of the current voice of the Father for their journey of healing, transformation, or restoration.

This material is a profound spiritual template for the reshaping and correcting of false identities and positions in the life of women, as the Father continues to bring forth both ancient and current revelatory perspectives in the reshaping and transformation of women back to the place of empowerment for our time.

You have the opportunity to begin again to understand and interact with the possibilities that heaven has invested in you. As you read and meditate on the valued principles, Tinashe has highlighted in this material. You feel awakened and emboldened through the power of the testimony shared here as your journey of spiritual rediscovery begins.

In this material, you will find your path and voice uniquely designed to be God's visionary warrior woman for your time. Please note that disenfranchisement is what we believe and accept when we have yet to discover and fully accept the Fatherhood of God in our lives. Therefore, in this material, although we all go through the deep emotional pain of either an abusive or absent father, it should not stop or cripple us from rising to become what our Heavenly Father ordained for us.

May you find the strength and courage in the testimony of the author, who has gone through many of what women find themselves in today but has decided not to remain beaten down by them. You can also choose to rise to the authority of the love and purpose of God for your life, as you use this book to encourage and empower yourself in the Lord. God has a plan for you.

Therefore, dare to dream God's dream for your life as you embrace all the Lord has ordained for. Indeed, you've been born for such a time.

- Isaiah-Phillips Akintola.

Foreword

As I journey on, slowly unravelling the beautiful mystery of God's purpose for my life, I have had the privilege of meeting many powerful women from different walks of life who have taken time to share their varying life lessons with me. Meeting many of these women has prompted me to believe that every woman is on a unique journey, and that we all have powerful stories to share. Another thing that I realized, through these different interactions and sharing of unique life stories, is that we are all Queens, destined to reign in our own unique calling, as the daughters of the most high King.

To be a Queen, however, is not about a position or a title. Queening is not about celebrating an idyllic reflection of ourselves, or making a big drama about our own person as we have (or may have) been otherwise socialized to believe. Queening is a celebration of all that is feminine, of womanhood/ sisterhood, of the strength and wisdom of the girl child. What is important and pivotal, however, is God: who He says we are as women, what He says we can do, and the purpose He has for our lives. It is not the crown that makes a Queen; it is the character, godly character, that is divinely crafted and nurtured.

To achieve what you were divinely created and equipped to be, you need to have a clear sense of identity. It is of utmost importance to realize and honor the Queen in you even before the world crowns you. You need to honor the gifts and talents God has placed within you through serving others, and that is what it means to be truly fulfilled. It means to be full and filled with the truth of who you are, and to let that truth of your authentic and divine nature radiate from the inside out.

The essence of womanhood lies in realizing and accepting God's value and anointing over your life. It is about taking pride in who and what God created you to be. I know pride may be considered a negative word, but I like Isak Dinesen's definition of pride. He says "Pride is having faith in the idea God had when He made you. A proud man (or woman) is conscious of the idea, and aspires to realize it. He (or she) does not strive towards happiness or comfort which may be irrelevant to God's idea of him (or her). His (or her) success is the idea of God successfully carried through."

Our growth in grace, our joy, our usefulness all depend upon our union with Christ. It is through communion with God that we can begin to understand, little by little, His divine plan for our lives and the true essence of womanhood.

As I take you through my life journey of self-realization, healing and becoming, I hope you (if you haven't already), will come to a full realization of the Queen in you. I hope you will discover the true essence of womanhood, and be inspired to take your own journey audaciously and courageously. I hope to inspire and stir in you the courage and boldness of Esther to wear your own crown with much pride and dignity.

Believe in your inner power. Own your story. Wear your crown with pride. Celebrate all that is majestic within you. Regardless of where you are positioned in life right now, always remember that all things are working together for your good, that God's purpose may be made manifest in and through your life. Let us, as women, take our rightful place, wear our royal robes and sit on our royal thrones. Once we own our true identity, we can then begin to build a true legacy of womanhood.

- Nashe

Introduction

There are so many courageous, faith-filled, action-packed, and breath-taking stories in the Bible; but to me, the story that stands out is that of Esther. It is a story that has grown, over the years, to be one of my favorites. A beautiful yet humble orphan girl, who was raised by her cousin as his own child, grows up to become a Queen and ends up saving a generation of her people through her faith and courage. I love this bible story particularly because it so beautifully illustrates how God created each and every one of us, uniquely and purposefully, and how we, especially as women, can fight our fears and bring glory to God.

This unforgettable story of courageous faith, in a unique way, reminds me of my own life story. It also, almost always, helps to remind me that God is busy with the completion of our salvation, and as crazy as it might seem, we all have a part to play in that story. I think that it is a story that is ripe for this generation and especially in this season. As the church, we are being called to unite and come together for the hour of our salvation draws near. As individuals, we are being called to walk into our purpose and take a courageous stand, declare our faith, and like Esther say, "If I perish I perish", but my faith will not be shaken.

In this book, I'd like to share with you lessons drawn from my own life, and may they be an encouragement for every woman out there; for those who, like Queen Esther, want to step out in faith into their divine calling, and those who want to experience something more of the power and presence of God. For with Gods help, we can do things we never could do on our own. As the apostle Paul writes, we can do all things through Christ's power, and our willingness to obey His word, His calling, and His plan for our lives.

I believe at one point or another in our lives, we can all relate to the story of Esther. As in all these heroic stories in the Bible and also our own lives, there is a pattern that we can draw. Firstly, there is always a call. God calls seemingly ordinary people to a certain task or purpose that requires extraordinary faith and trust. Secondly, in each story, there is always fear or an element of doubt. We question our ability to achieve the task that God has called us to. At times, we are afraid to fail, or like Esther, we are even afraid to die if we attempt to do that task. Thirdly, there is always a decision, either to accept God's call or to deny it; but always, people must decide. Lastly, there is always a changed life or lives. Those who say yes to Gods call are forever changed, and also the lives they touch. As Oswald Chambers once wrote, "If you give God the right to yourself, he will make a holy experiment out of you, and God's experiments always succeed." But firstly, we must say yes to God's call, and only then can He begin to work in and through us.

I believe that this pattern from Scripture continues today. There is a purpose for your life to which God is calling you, and when you say yes to His calling, it sets in motion a divine dynamic far beyond mere human power. Maybe it has to do with your work, or a relational risk, a gift you could develop, or resources you could give. Perhaps it will involve an act of courage and facing your deepest fear. Certainly, it will go to the core of who you are and what you do.

So, together, in this book, we are going on a journey. And as we go through that journey I hope we not only learn to trust God, but we also learn to hear His call, to transcend fear and doubt, and to risk everything in faith. My hope is that you dont simply read this book, but that it prompts you to say yes to Gods call.

Nashe -With God- The journey of a Transformed woman

Chapter 1: Woman on a Mission

A journey of purposeful living and discovering your destiny

"The only service you can render God is to give expression to what He is trying to give the world, through you. The only service
you can render God is to make the very most of yourself in order that God may live in you to the utmost of your possibilities."
- Wallace D. Wattles,

Every day, you and I take another step of our life journey on this planet, making our way through this vast universe. We only get one trip and so I am determined to make it count and live a life worth remembering. I long to live the purposeful life that God has intended for me and I bet you do too; but it's a pretty uncertain ride sometimes, and it seems a constant battle between fear and faith in each undertaking. Life is often unpredictable and comes with many trials and tribulations, but, take heart, you're not alone.

My story, like every human story, is, at least in part, a struggle between faith and fear. It is a story about overcoming doubt and living out God's plan. It is about living an audacious life and becoming the person that I was predestined to become. That is what I believe is my life mission, and in fulfilling it, I hope to inspire other women to take a stand and do the same. Because of this, I have found myself drawn to the story of Esther. As I mentioned earlier, the story of Esther has, over the years, grown to be one of my favorites. The Bible book of Esther is a dramatic account which can give us insight into Gods special and purposeful plan for our lives. The story gives us many powerful lessons about purpose, courage, divine timing, and Gods supreme love. All these lessons I have learnt in and through my own life as well.

In the following chapters, I will share with you my life story, and as you go through each moment, I hope it teaches you something about purpose, faith and courage. But to begin with, lets get an aerial overview. What goes into living a purposeful life? What does it take to fulfill your life mission? Here are a few lessons I learnt from Queen Esther, that have, in no small part, contributed to the woman I am today, and are foundational to the woman I wish to become.

Courage:

First and foremost, it takes courage to live an authentic, purpose driven life. Imagine being Esther, hearing God's call to stand in the gap and intercede for a generation, but you consider the risk: facing Xerxes the Persian king at the height of his power and knowing that an attempt to do so might get you killed. What would you do? Perhaps you could've easily declined knowing fully well that it wasn't your life in danger anyway, knowing that no one would dare touch the queen. At the same time, you also know that if you don't do what God has called you to do, there is a great chance that someone's life will be at stake. Let me tell you a secret, if you didn't know it already: Someone, somewhere in this world is waiting for you and for me to do what God has called us to do.

Queen Esther acted courageously when she made the decision to gather the house of Israel, fast and approach the king. She had courage to plan the feasts and good timing to make her requests. She further had courage to beg King Ahasuerus to save Israel after Haman's demise, and make further requests.

Courage breeds courage. Courage is something we can all build, like muscle. The more we practice it, the more confidence and boldness we have. The truly amazing things in life come when we step out of our comfort zone, but to do so, we must have courage.

There is something - Someone inside us who tells us there is more to life than living in our comfort zones. Like Esther, we all have to leave the certainty and comforts of our 'Palace' and step out in courageous faith and obedience to God's call. You were made for something more. God is calling you to more. There is something inside you that wants to leave the comfort of routine existence and abandon to the high adventure of heeding to God's calling in your life. Why don't you trust that instinct, and follow Christ?

Let me ask you a very important question: What are you afraid of? Your 'Persian king' is whatever you fear to face in your life apart from God himself. Your 'Palace' is whatever you are tempted to put your trust in, especially when life gets a little rough. It is whatever keeps you so comfortable that you don't want to give it up even if it is keeping you from fulfilling your purpose. It could be a relationship, a job or even a persona you have created for yourself. Your comfort zone is whatever pulls you away from the high adventure of extreme discipleship. It is time to leave that comfort zone, boldly TAKE COURAGE AND FULFILL YOUR PURPOSE!

Faith:

One of the more, if not most important ingredients to living a purposeful life is FAITH. Faith is confidence in God's miracle-working power. It is foundational to the Christian walk. As the author of Hebrews poetically writes in the bible: "It is

impossible to please God without faith."

Courage works hand in hand with faith. Faith is the ability to trust God, to surrender all doubt and say "I do not know how I am going to do this, but I believe that God will make a way and see me through."

Queen Esther's initiative to gather the people of Israel in prayer and fasting, before initiating a talk with the king without being summoned, was an act of great faith. It takes faith to do the seemingly impossible. To believe that the impossible is possible, one must take a leap of faith and it doesn't matter who you are or what you do. Whether one is an entrepreneur, aspiring parent, or future Noble Prize Laureate, one must take a leap of faith. You cannot achieve the impossible without faith.

It is only through faith that we can reach the recesses of Godly character, and only then can the fruits of the spirit be made manifest in us. Love, joy, peace, long suffering, gentleness, faith, meekness, and temperance. Action:

When Mordechai discovered Haman's plan to destroy the
Israelites, he enlisted Esther's help, asking her to go before the King
and beg him, on behalf of her people, to save them. Esther, after wrestling
her doubt to exhaustion, finally devised the plan of how to actually face
up to the King and ask him to spare her people from Haman's cruel plot.

It was her initiative to gather her people and request them to fast for
three days, as a form of repentance in the face of the possible impending
tragedy. It was also by her design that she initiated two feasts before
making her request from the king.

An idea with no action is meaningless. A plan without the ability
to take initiative will not bear fruit. Had Esther not carefully carved a
strategic plan of action and taken the initiative to see it through, we
probably would be telling a different tale today. Taking action is what
separates disciple and spectator. We are called to be disciples and to live
a Godly life. Discipleship is in no way passive. It is a call to action, to
growth; and growth does not occur where there is no action.

Your faith will not bear any fruit if you don't take action. Believing
you can achieve without stepping out and doing what needs to be done
will not change anything in your life.

Chapter 2: From humble beginnings

"Although you started with little you will end with much"
- Job 8vs7

God has always been in the business of doing much with little. We see this time and time again, in so many stories in the Bible. He inspires those who believe to do the impossible: like when Gideon chased down and conquered an army in the hundreds of thousands with only 300 men; or when teenaged David faced up to, and slew GIANT Goliath with a sling; and even when Jesus himself fed the multitude with only five loaves and two fish! All these stories are so surreal, right?

I believe this is how God always shows us His grace and unmatched miracle-working power. God always equips seemingly ordinary people to do extraordinary deeds for the purpose of His glory to be made manifest. I imagine this to be the case in Esther's story: a young woman born into a family of Jewish exiles, orphaned at an early age, and from the smallest tribe in all of Israel, (the tribe of Benjamin). Who could imagine a mere orphaned maiden who came from such a lowly place to be the one God uses to intercede for the salvation of an entire nation?

Our lives take a similar pattern. It might be difficult to see the ending from the beginning. You might not see the uniqueness of your life story from where you are standing. It might be difficult to understand God's purpose through your everyday life experience but, believe me, God is positioning and setting you up for a much greater purpose than you can think or imagine.

***

My name is Tinashe, which, loosely translated, could mean 'God is with us' or 'we are with God'. Looking back, I feel that my name was a prophetic declaration over my life, because I believe my journey has been one taken one step at a time "Nashe" (with God).

I was born on the 8th of March in 1989, the first in a family of four children, in a city in the southern part of Zimbabwe called Bulawayo. The greater part of my childhood and early adolescent years were, however, spent in a small town in the central part of Zimbabwe called Gweru, where I made a lot of my childhood memories, a place that will always feel like home to me.

My family was very religious, and this was, by a large part, due to my mother's encouragement. I grew up on the wings of my mother's faith. She played an integral part in my journey of spiritual growth. My mother was, however, as with most parents, a complicated human being, quite contradictory at times: moralistic but also a devout lover of pleasure, deeply religious but seemingly quite secular. She would enjoy her church services just as much as she would a nice party on the town. She was passionate about everything she did. My father, in contrast, seemed to be quite indifferent. He was an enigma of sorts and quite hard to read. He wasn't religious and would go to church occasionally only as a gesture to appease my mother's religious persuasions.

We were devout Catholics (at least my mother was), my mother would have it no other way. As evidence, you could see crucifixes, pictures of Jesus and Mary the virgin mother, and rosaries carefully placed in different corners and shelves of our home.

My mother would teach me how to pray. She insisted, from an early age, that I cross myself (doing the sign of the crucifix, as is custom for Catholics), and offer a prayer for my food before I ate it. Some days, when she wasn't too tired after work, she would invite us, my sibling Tavonga and I (there was just the two of us then before my two youngest siblings were born) to her bedroom to say a little prayer before we went to bed. I remember even when we had fallen on hard times, my mother would encourage us to pray. She believed that God would see us through, no matter what. Looking back, I realize that all this helped me to overcome so many trying seasons and moments in my life. My mother taught me that prayer was key to solving all of life's problems. Whether in doubt, in pain, in fear, in discomfort, or discouraged, prayer was her answer. I learnt at an early age the power of prayer, even though at the time I did not fully comprehend the depth and breadth of how to and what it meant to pray.

From as early as I can remember, we would go to church services almost every Sunday and since then, for me, Sundays seem 'incomplete' without church. We would rarely miss church; my mother would not have it. Church was something she took very seriously. Every Sunday morning, she would wake us up early, make porridge and bath my younger sibling and I until we were sparkling clean. You could tell we were bathed thoroughly because you could spot our beaming foreheads from a distance. Our faces would be radiant, not because of our gleeful childish smiles, but because of the generous amount of Blue Seal Vaseline (petroleum jelly) applied to our faces. She would dress us up in our Sunday best and we would be on our way.

Being late for church was something my mother abhorred. She would wake us up very early on most Sundays to make sure we were all ready and on time. If you were not done by the time she was ready to leave, you would be forced to finish dressing up in the car on the way to church, or risk being left behind. If you were unfortunate enough to be left behind on any particular Sunday, you would anxiously wait to get a good beating (what kids today call a 'spanking'), once she returned. If there is one thing my mother was an expert at, it was giving beatings. Growing up, I'm sure every child thinks their mother gives the worst beatings, but my mother's were the worst! Believe me when I say she was an expert at delivering a good hiding. She was so skilled in the art that anything in her hand or around her could be used to deliver a swift spanking. Be it a slipper on her foot or a wooden cooking spoon, anything in her hands was lethal. My mother would literally and figuratively thrash you; she would whoop you until the 'mischief-causing devil' in you was exorcised. No amount of tears could save you. There were no negotiations to be had and no manipulations were tolerated.

I remember sometimes, when my younger brother or I were caught doing a little mischief, my mother would drag you into her bedroom, pull out her huge leather bound Bible and ask you to open it to the book of Proverbs 13vs 24, and read: Whoever spares the rod hates his son, but he who loves him is diligent to discipline him. After reading that verse, you knew exactly what was coming next: a good beating.

At church, we would go with the rest of the children to Sunday school, unless there was a special mass and Sunday school was canceled. Mass is the word Catholics use for church services. On days when Sunday school was canceled, we would attend the regular service with our mother and the rest of the adults in the main church building. My mother had a favorite pew she liked to sit in. Whenever she attended services, she would sit, always, in the front pew at the extreme right of the huge church auditorium. She always sat right in the front of the church, and no matter how late we were, she would march us straight to the front of the church. You couldn't, wouldn't, dare object. If you tried to object, my mother had this thing she would do, this look she would give you from the corner of her eye, and that particular look was enough to set you straight. It was a look we had grown to understand and learnt to immediately obey, like an unvoiced command, or face the consequence - which was usually a good beating. The look had many shades of meaning; it could mean stop whatever you are doing, behave yourself or don't try me, but the bottom line was pretty clear.

***

A purpose revealed

When there was no special mass, we would go to Sunday school. I enjoyed my time at Sunday school immensely. We would read bible stories and sing songs. It was there that I realized a deep desire within me for the love of the Lord, and in the ensuing years, I would soon learn that my greatest purpose in life is to make Him loved, through sharing the love that He has carefully placed within me.

Earlier in my life, I was very outgoing, outspoken, naturally optimistic and I had a determined spirit (I believe I'm still many of those things presently). I was always talking and asking questions. I remember I would almost always be on the noisemakers list, because I would rarely keep quiet. One of the teachers at Sunday school decided to put my talking to good use, and started asking me to sing or share a bible verse that I had committed to memory, with the other children. I was never one to shy away from such tasks. I would sing and recite memorized Bible verses with so much energy. I quickly gained a reputation in Sunday school for my zeal and determination, which landed me a leadership role. This would also continue to happen throughout my high-school and college years.

During the Sunday school services, I started being tasked with reading a verse from the Bible and sharing a few words of encouragement. I would give short talks about fellowship with God and whatever else I would feel placed on my heart to share. Even though I was still young and probably not an eloquent enough speaker, my peers and classmates were evidently moved by my words. They responded well to my teachings. It appeared to touch something within them. I realize now that slowly, God was positioning me for His purpose at a tender age, and this lit sparks of passion that He had placed within me.

Many people, both young and old alike, struggle to find their purpose in life. They struggle to find meaning and direction in their lives. They struggle with self-worth, because they are not clear on how they can contribute and make a difference in the world.

I believe purpose is something that we are born into. Our purpose is rooted deep within us. But to get really clear on what God is calling us to do, we need to pursue God's love and get to know Him personally. Pray, read His Word and meditate on it. To know God and believe in Him is the best thing that can happen to your life. He is the author and finisher of our faith. He can transform your life and bring out success from your failures, strength from your weakness and beauty from your ashes.

Looking back, I see how God uniquely gifted, nurtured and prepared me for my purpose in all the challenges and pain that I went through. These are the scars of my purpose.

You will know you have found your passion when your talents, focus, commitment and knowledge all come together in a way that excites you. When you find your purpose, your work and pleasure become one and the same. Your passion will lead you to your purpose, and both are activated when you use your gifts and talents in the service of others. You are custom-made for a purpose, as am I. Every part of you - from your mental, physical and spiritual strengths to your life experiences and gifts, are part and parcel of a unique package that is you. They are all designed to fulfill your God-given purpose.

People sometimes romanticize the notion of finding their purpose or calling in life. Receiving a calling from God is not the same thing as falling into your dream career. A dream career generally promises wealth, power, status, security, and great benefits. Finding one's purpose is a different story altogether. It is never as glamorous as we hope, it never comes at a convenient time, and usually, it seems impossible.

I was baptized at an early age as is custom for all children born in the Catholic Church. It was my mother's wish that all her children be baptized and dedicated to the Lord. Soon after, I went for catechism lessons. These were like induction lessons that you had to go through to become a bona fide catholic. After I had completed the lessons, I was officially a catholic and could finally serve in the church. My mother, true to her nature, wasted no time, as a few weeks after that, she signed me up to be one of two people who read the Bible in church. I remember only hearing of it at the end of the church service during the announcements segment. She was always encouraging me to step out of my comfort zone in small, and sometimes big ways - something that I presently appreciate, because life is never truly lived in our comfort zones. We need to step out and step into God's calling and purpose for our lives, just as Esther was called up into the king's harem to be set apart for her purpose. Likewise, God is busy preparing you for His work to serve as a vessel of His love.

Chapter 3: Growing Pains

"He who began a good work in you will finish it until the day of Jesus Christ." **Philippians 1vs6**

Growing up is never a painless process as one would imagine or wish it to be. In fact, growth is often painful. It is a struggle to be, and also to become. Growth is also never linear. There is no straight line to maturity (spiritually, psychologically or otherwise). It is usually like walking on a winding trail with no end in sight. There are as many wrong turns as right ones along the way, and sometimes (or rather most times), it is hard to tell which is which. You are forced to make a decision and sometimes you are not always in the right, but that doesn't have to stop you. You try and try again. The only way you can find the right path is when you follow Jesus, who is the way, the truth and the life. But that too doesn't empty life of its troubles. It does, however, help in finding the meaning through the pain.

***

My mother, being a firm catholic, thought it would be best for us (my younger brother and I) to attend catholic schools. I attended an all-girls high school called Regina Mundi; a strict boarding school run by nuns.

During my high school years, I remember being part of a youth fellowship group and we usually met on Sunday afternoons. This was a convenient time for all the members since most of us would be free around that time. Such meetings were mandatory and everyone was expected to attend one group or another during Sunday afternoons. I would certainly enjoy those few hours of fellowship: sharing the word of God, singing praise songs, and sharing prayer requests. I remember, once in a while, someone would share a testimony of an answered prayer. All this would strengthen my faith and encourage me to pray more fervently and diligently.

My spiritual growth during this period of my life wasn't a straight line. If I am being completely honest, it was more of a roller-coaster ride. It was a struggle marked by many highs and lows. Though I had been given the grace to know about Christ at an early age, I was yet to master how to constantly and consistently commune with Him, and how to surrender my life completely to Him.

High school came with new challenges. Your teenage years are usually the time when you become aware of your differences and then, as you grow older, you spend the rest of your life realizing how much we are all similar to each other. This period can be challenging for anyone, as everyone, at that stage is trying to figure out how to fit in, where to fit in and what the future holds for them.

Like the typical teenager, I struggled to fit in. I always felt like a square peg in a round hole. I felt as if I had an identity crisis. High school is a time when you need to figure out who you are as a person and establish an individual identity. In the end, I chose being popular over being authentic. I would choose friends based on their popularity and not based on their character.

When you are younger, outside approval weighs more to you, than self-approval. What we do not realize is that, every time we seek outside approval, we compromise our own integrity.

At the time, I was self-conscious, and in need of someone to tell me that I was enough just the way I was. I had no tools to deal with my anxiety. I carried deep trauma, shame and fear – from growing up with a violent and abusive father.

For a time, during adolescence and into my early adult life, I struggled to speak up for myself. On the outside, I seemed quite confident and self-assured, but it was a facade behind which I hid my insecurities. I struggled to set boundaries with other people, and it constantly led to people taking advantage of me. All of it was deeply rooted in fear. I spent all of my energy hiding and keeping the struggles of my life a secret, as I was ashamed of sharing the pain of my not-so-picture-perfect life. I carried this dysfunction with me in lonely silence.

As a teenager trying to come to terms with the trauma of my past, I made the mistake of thinking that no one else hurt like I did and that my problems were insurmountable. I thought that the challenges I faced were unique, that I couldn't share my burdens, even with those who loved and cared for me.

Sometimes when I think back to my teenage years, I find myself close to tears, not because I feel sorry for myself, but because I mourn the comfort I could not give myself back then. I mourn the girl who felt so lost and did not understand what was happening or why. I mourn the parents who were ill equipped to handle my insecurities, and could not give me the comfort I needed. I mourn for so many other girls who, like me, struggle in the same way today.

When you are young, everything seems so important, as life and death. It is difficult to be grateful when you are constantly griping, wishing for and wanting more. The biggest reason for this is that we tend to overvalue what we dont have and undervalue what we do. The only antidote to this is gratitude. Gratitude is key to living an authentic life.

I really did not feel like I belonged anywhere, I always felt so alone. It is during this period, unknown to me at the time, that I embarked on a life long journey of soul searching, to figure out who I was, what I liked, what I believed in, and what I wanted in life. Because I did not know how to ask these questions clearly, the answers remained elusive, and the help I so desperately needed was nowhere to be found. I began to hide, not physically, but I slowly became emotionally unavailable. It was a coping strategy I slowly picked up over the years.

It is around this time that I joined the drama club. I remember thinking that finally, I had found something that I was really good at. The thing about acting is that it allows you to hide in plain sight, because you can be anything or anyone, as long as you can play the part. This philosophy spilled over into my real life too. Because I was struggling with my identity, I settled for role playing. It is easier to pretend that you are something other than yourself when you don't know who and what you are; and when you pretend long enough, separating the two entities becomes hard. I believe identity is at the heart of living a purpose-driven and God-centered life. But because we are often running away and hiding from who we are, it is difficult and almost impossible to know the purpose God has for our lives. To have a real and honest encounter with God, you have to show up as your real self, and only then can God reveal Himself to you. It is when you open up to him and let go of all that you are not, that He can guide you into the totality of who you are.

What I did not realize at the time was that being alone was not the same thing as being lonely. Because I felt so alone, I ended up hanging with the wild kids, and I would engage in different self-destructive activities, in an attempt to feel like I belonged. It was cool back then to be part of a clique, even though I knew deep down that I did not belong. It was a good place to hide, or so I thought.

When we are younger, we strive to fit in, when what God has called us to do is stand out. It is always scary to stand out, but it is always necessary. Paul sums it up nicely when he says that though we are in this world, we are not of this world. We are not born to fit in or conform to the status quo, but we are born to stand out. We all want to feel like we belong somewhere, to something or even to someone. What we do not realize is that, it is during the alone times that God reveals himself to us and leads us to spiritual maturity.

Enoch walked with God alone. Noah preached and built the ark alone. Moses ascended Sinai alone. David fought Goliath alone. Elijah sacrificed on Mount Carmel alone, against a multitude of Baal's prophets. Esther, crying 'if I perish I perish', faced the king alone. It might seem that all these people were alone, but in reality, the faithful servant of God is never alone, because God is always with them.

When you fully receive God's love and approval, you receive the freedom to be yourself. You do not wait for people to accept you or validate you because you know you are somebody. That freedom can only be found when we commune with God, who is the author and finisher, not only of our faith, but of our lives too.

I realized there is a connection between fellowship with God and how we see our lives and ourselves. When we break fellowship with God, it disrupts how we see ourselves. We become misaligned with our Creator, who is the true source of our identity and purpose. This is evident in the world today. An alarming number of people are suffering from mental health and related issues, a clear sign of broken fellowship with God. A growing number (especially during the teenage years) also struggle with body image issues and this is all because we have lost oneness with our creator. When you are in fellowship with God, you become more aware of who you are, who you can be, and your purpose. You grow into spiritual maturity, and you believe and fully embrace that you are 'enough'. You know intrinsically and without a doubt that your body is enough, and your life is complete, divine and unique. You believe that you are a masterpiece in progress. You do not just affirm that you are fearfully and wonderfully made, but you live it and wholeheartedly believe it!

I came to the realization that I needed to own my identity. Once I accepted that God loved me and had a purpose for me, my self-image changed and so did my attitude and my actions. It did not happen overnight however. It was a gradual process that was marked by many highs and lows. You might be going through the same struggles. If you are, maybe I can share a few words of wisdom that helped to remind me of who I was and what I could achieve.

You are a child of God. He created you. You may see yourself as imperfect, but God does not. You were made according to His plan. If you treat others with respect and kindness, if you try to do the right things and to make the most of your gifts, you will be worthy of love.

To be loved by others, you must first love yourself. If you come from love, there is no need to look for it elsewhere. If you find it difficult to love yourself, then you have work to do before you can expect anyone else to sign on to a relationship with you.

Growth is often an uncomfortable journey into better versions of ourselves. In the process, we lose old redundant parts of ourselves and gain others. The tragedy we have as the church today is that many people try to mimic spiritual growth, and they are pretty good at pretending.

You can't pretend your way to spiritual growth. No matter how many years ago you were born again, it is not a right to spiritual maturity. Authentic growth happens organically and it is also something evident. True, authentic spiritual growth is achieved when you learn that it is not the blessing you need but the blesser, that it is not the provision you seek but the provider, that it is not the saving you are after but the Savior, and that it is not the gift you need but the giver. True growth is when you understand that God is your every need, He is the wellspring of living water, and He will meet you at your point of need.

***

During this period of my struggle with identity and purpose in high school, my parents were facing a different kind of struggle at home. My parents' relationship had slowly broken down and had grown violent and abusive.

My mother was what I would call, for lack of a better phrase, 'a married single-mother'. She would take care of my siblings and I, and make sure we had everything that we needed, from food, clothes and even our tuition. My father was scarcely available. As a child, I barely had a relationship with my father, he never had an active presence in my life. He was never there for me in the way I needed him to be. Even though he would be there physically, he was not accessible emotionally and spiritually. This created a distance between us and slowly but surely, fueled by all the physical and emotional abuse we endured at his hands, that distance began to turn into resentment and hatred.

I have very few memories of my father, and of those few, I have even fewer good ones. I remember watching my father beating up my mother this one morning before school. He was dragging her through the house, and she was bleeding from her mouth, the nightie she was wearing covered in blood. I remember screaming at my dad as tears ran down my face, begging him to stop. I ran and grabbed his leg and tried to bite him, but he just pushed me away. Minutes later, after everything had quieted down, he ordered my younger brother and I to go to school. We had not even had breakfast yet, and our lunch for school had not even been prepared. We just marched out of the house with no bus fare or anything. I remember a kind neighbor taking us to school that day. He used to drive his grandkids to school in his brownish old Peugeot. The school his grandchildren attended was reasonably close to ours, so on days when we were lucky to meet him before he left, he would give us a ride. This is one of my earliest memories of my parents' fights.

Before this, I would see my mother with a bloodshot eye or a swollen cheek, and I would ask what had happened. She would lie and tell me that she had fallen or something. Though still a child, I could tell this was not true.

The abuse got worse and worse over time. My father would get drunk and beat my mother and if we cried, he would beat up my little brother and I too. On the surface, no one could tell what we were going through, we looked like a nice, happy family from the suburbs. Deep down, however, we were battling and struggling with abuse. Everything finally took a turn one day when my mother had had enough. I remember her coming to pick me up from school one afternoon, nose bandaged up, and eyes red. It looked like she had been crying. She did not say much to me, but I was sure something was up because midweek school visits were not a common occurrence. I soon learned that early that morning, my parents had gotten into an argument and a fight had broken out. My father bit my mother's nose and tore out a chunk. This was the second time such an incident was happening, the first time being when he had bitten her bottom lip. After getting medical attention and receiving advice from some of her friends, she had taken a restraining order against my father.

All this, to say the least, was a very traumatic experience for me. I remember my father moving out of the house. My mother took everything that was in the house, hired a truck and sent the property to my father, who was now renting a house somewhere we never visited. The air, the atmosphere around the house seemed different then. It was as if there was a newly found freedom, as though a weight had been removed. It is then I realized when you are living in an abusive environment, you often feel like you have no freedom. You struggle with selfexpression and you are always doubtful and even suspicious when you experience moments of joy.

****

Death in the family

My siblings and I had to adjust to the new living arrangements after our parents separated. We never traveled to see my father, but once in a while, he would come to the house and have lunch with us. I assumed it was to see us (his children), but he never spoke with us or said much at all. We would exchange greetings and goodbyes and that was that.

My father's visits started getting fewer and fewer, but I barely noticed it. My mother would sometimes tell us what she heard from the rumor mill. One day she came home and told me that my father had started living with his new girlfriend. I felt indifferent about it at the time. I really did not care much for my father because I felt he did not care much for my siblings and I, either.

A few months down the line, my father fell ill. At first, he just complained about having minor headaches at work. Then he started complaining about general body weakness and feeling fatigued all the time. Over time, his illness got worse, to the point where he had to be hospitalized. My mother would take us to see him often and we would exchange pleasantries, and ask how he was doing. He would say he was okay and getting better, but I always thought he was just trying to put on a brave face for us. Slowly, his illness got worse and worse. Since my father was staying alone at the time, one of my uncles came to take care of him. My uncle decided it was better to nurse him at home because the doctors had said they could not do much for him at the hospital, and he could return home and take his medication while he recovered.

On most weekends, my mother would take my siblings and I to see our father. I remember on one of the last trips we went to see him, he did not remember who we were. My father could not recognize us, his children! He had grown sickly thin and had developed squinted eyes. He could not do anything for himself, he had to be wheeled to the restroom and bathed. He was a pale shadow of the man he used to be.

My father was a tall, dark man with an average build. He was intelligent and charming. The man I saw sleeping on a hospital bed that day did not even remotely resemble the man I remembered my father to be.

My father soon passed away. I was at school when he passed on, and a cousin who used to stay with us at home came to pick me up from school. I suspected something was wrong because midweek school visits were unusual. I asked my cousin what was going on, but he did not tell me anything. I remember getting home and my mother telling me that my father had died. In that moment, I had so many thoughts going through my mind. I had mixed emotions; I didn't know how to feel at the time. My heart was grieving, but my mind was filled with anger. I cried and mourned the loss of my father. Though we did not have a smooth relationship, he was still my father, and for that, I was and still am eternally grateful.

Losing a parent is never easy, even when you have a rough relationship like I had with my father. It is still painful.

My mother and uncles made arrangements for my father's funeral. We traveled to our rural home in Nyanga for the burial. It was a day's trip from Gweru, and the next day was the scheduled date for my father's burial. At about noon, the funeral procession proceeded to the village cemetery where, as is customary, a eulogy and testimonials were shared by different people who knew my father. After the testimonials, one of my uncles stood up to read what he said was my father's dying letter. In the letter were my father's supposed 'dying wishes'. Midway through the reading of the letter, my mother's relatives started to leave, a sign of disagreement with the letter. They suspected the letter to have been forged by one of my uncles in a bid to control his late brother's estate. I remember a part of the letter were my father denied paternity of my siblings and I. Although I was still young, I can never forget that part. It hurt me deeply to think that my own father would deny us, his own children.

***

In the Bible, in the book of Isaiah, God says, I will not cause pain without allowing something new to be born (Isaiah 66vs9). Pain is usually a precursor to something new. It opens us up to newer and sometimes even better versions of ourselves. Like labor pains, all our struggles are there to birth something new within us.

Sometimes we try, usually, in vain to step over our struggles. We try to hide our pain and sweep it under the carpet, but soon enough it all catches up to us, and resurfaces in the soul. I believe that we shouldn't try to step over our struggles if it is necessary to pass under them. To pass under is to go through the difficulties life throws at you. It means to live with the struggles and deal with them interiorly, it means to carry your cross, because struggles and difficulties contain the hidden meaning of our future.

I have met a lot of people who try to hide from their pain, who try to deny that their reality is painful, who are afraid to confront life head on. Usually, these people try to appear spiritually transcendent but behind their façade, their worlds are crumbling. Whatever pain you have gone through or are still going through, consider these labor pains. God is busy preparing you for something new. As God promised Joshua, "I will be with you: I will not fail you, nor will I forsake you" (Joshua 1:5). So be strong and courageous, as you go through the difficult seasons in your life, for it is for your growth and transformation.

Chapter 4: Beauty for Ashes

"God makes everything beautiful for its own time." **Ecclesiastes 3 VS 11**

I imagine when Esther was called to the palace, her whole life took a dramatic turn. Everything she knew and was accustomed to had changed. She was taken away from what was familiar and thrust into new territory. She was separated from her friends, her family and everything she was used to. I imagine she must have felt scared, lonely and shocked. Probably this was her first time away from home. This is what happens when God wants to elevate you. He singles you out and separates you from all that is familiar to you. With the careful precision of a farmer who sifts the wheat from the husks, God will strip you away from everything you know so that all you have to rely on is Him. He will separate you from your past and all that is familiar. That is how he prunes us so that we may bear much fruit for His kingdom.

***

I was in my second year of university when my mother got seriously ill. She had been to many places seeking treatment, getting medical and spiritual attention but nothing seemed to help. In those days, she had just moved in with her new partner. My two youngest siblings were also staying with her. I remember confronting my mother about such living arrangements because I worried much about my younger sisters, but she assured me everything was fine.

I had to take leave from school for a while to take care of my ailing mother and my siblings. Things took a drastic turn and about three weeks after my move home, my mother succumbed to her illness and passed on. At that moment, my whole world came to a standstill. I felt so lost and afraid and a part of me blamed God. How could a benevolent and caring God take my only surviving parent, the only person who made sure I had enough to eat? So many questions I could not find answers to flooded my mind. What was I going to do? How would I take care of my siblings? I had no money, no job and my mother's business was on its knees due to the many months of her absence. I literally had no place to start. If there was any 'rock bottom' moment in my life story, this was probably it.

I remember thinking my life had turned out exactly like in one movie I watched when I was younger. It was a movie called Everyone's child, written and directed by Tsitsi Dangarembga. It was a story about children who were orphaned at a young age and were left wandering alone, with no one to help them. That is what was happening to me at that moment. We (my siblings and I) literally had nowhere to go and nothing to see us through at that time.

My mother was my everything. She was my only support through thick and thin. During the month she got seriously ill, she had started opening up to me like she had never before. We never had one on one conversations about life and stuff like that, but the few months before her death were different. As I mentioned before, six years earlier, my father had passed on. I did not know at the time that he had succumbed to HIV/Aids related illness. I also did not know, though I strongly suspected, that after my father passed away, my mother went and got tested, and was found positive too. She later confided in me about her illness and much more. Though I knew it all, it still did not help to prepare me for her death. I had always thought about what it would be like if my mother were to die, and I would mentally rehearse it; but nothing, absolutely nothing can prepare you for the death of your loved one.

There was so much to do and so little to go by. My mother's relatives and family members came to the funeral. Her friends and colleagues also came for the burial. Through all this, I was just in so much shock and denial. I felt as though this was one long bad dream and soon, I would wake up and it would all be over.

After my mother's funeral, my mother's relatives decided it would be best to separate us because no one person could take on the responsibility of taking care of all of us. I resisted this arrangement because I felt my little sisters were still too young. I feared they would suffer from neglect. Not that my mother's family are bad people, no! On the contrary, they are very supportive, but I felt it would be best if they remained together. At the same time, I did not have the capacity to care of them myself. There are times you just want to ask God and say "God, you said you have a plan for me. I think this is a pretty good time to be sharing that plan because honestly, I am at my wits' end." This was one of those moments for me, I didn't know what to do. But I knew I had to finish school. That was the only way I could be of any help to my family, I thought.

One day, my mother's friend invited me over to her office. She said she could assist me with applying for a stand. The government was allocating housing stands to vulnerable and marginalized groups in society. Safe to say, we fit the bill. On my way there, I was so lost in my thoughts and so stressed out. I remember bumping into one lady who greeted me by name and went on to pass her condolences on the loss of my mother. After that, she told me about a program that was assisting orphans and other disadvantaged children to pay their tuition. She gave me the address and phone number of the place, and I promised I would check it out after my scheduled meeting. I thanked her and we parted ways.

As soon as my appointment was done, I rushed straight to the office I had been directed to. Indeed, they were there. I was met by a gracious young lady who proceeded to explain to me in detail about the Capernaum Trust program and how they go about their business. I narrated our situation to her; that my sisters had no one to care of them while I was away. They told me I needed to go to Harare (which is the capital city of Zimbabwe) to their headquarters to explain my special request that my sisters be assisted not only in paying their school fees, but also their boarding fees. I took my sisters' report books from school and my parents' deaths certificates, and I went to Harare, to the Capernaum Trust Foundation headquarters. Along the way, I was offering a silent prayer, hoping my sisters would be accepted into the program. I got to Harare and headed straight to the headquarters and explained my situation. They understood me and said they were paying school fees and boarding fees for students who were excelling and had trouble at home, so that they could focus more on their studies. I quickly pulled out my little sisters' report books and handed them over, knowing secretly that my prayers had been answered. They opened each one of them and just a few pages into each, they were quickly impressed. They agreed to pay my sisters tuition! I was filled with so much joy and comfort. The Lord had come through for me when I needed Him the most. I was asked to fill out some forms and then bring copies of my parents' death certificates, my sisters' birth certificates, as well as information about where they were currently schooling.

Later, I returned to the place where I had met the lady who told me about the Capernaum trust. I went to the government complex building where I had met her, asked around the offices where I could find her, but to my surprise, no one knew her name. I described what she looked like but still no one knew her. I left the place confused. I returned to the place a couple more times to find her, but still, nothing. At that moment, I knew deep within me that I had been visited by an angel. I was so convinced of this, because absolutely no one knew the lady that I had spoken to. I looked for her everywhere using the office details she had given me, but no one knew who she was. She had appeared in my time of need, strengthened me and helped me. The Bible talks about how angels are ministering spirits that help us in our time of need and this made me pretty certain that this lady was an angel.

.... Once you become aware of your own powerlessness your imperfections and above all accept yourself as you are. God can begin to show himself to you as one who is ready to help and provide for all your needs. In the beginning of every Christian walk we aspire to love the lord but in the end we soon understand it is enough to be loved by him.

Though this was a trying time in my life, the Lord stood by me as he did with Paul, and strengthened me.

I remember reading the verse that talks about God bringing beauty from your ashes, and I highlighted it in my Bible and would often share it with my friends. But I think I never understood what was at the heart of that verse. For there to be ashes, firstly, something has to burn. And I always seemed to miss that part. After the burning and nothing is left but the cold ashes of what was, God will bring out your beauty! He will make you anew, mold you and fashion you into a vessel fit for His purpose, from whatever is left after your past has been burnt away. Whatever you may be going through, always remember that when God takes something or someone from your life, it is for your pruning. If you keep holding onto and weeping over the ashes, you will miss the new thing that He is about to do for you, through you and in you.

***

A grief deferred

The death of my mother left a huge hole inside my soul that only God's love could fill. Because I had so much to think about and do, I had no time to grieve and heal. I spent most of my time between making funeral arrangements for my mother's burial and settling her estate. After my mother's burial, I returned to school. Because I had been absent for so long, I had a lot to do and a lot to catch up on. Slowly, unknowingly, I began to fill the hole in my soul with anger, bitterness and hate. All those negative emotions began to eat me up inside. My relationships with friends and family began to suffer as a result of my pain and grief. I was bitter, I was in pain. I would not admit it at the time, but I really felt as though God had let me down. For a brief time, I shut God out of my life because I was angry. I could not accept He loved me until I realized that everything He does has a reason.

One thing I have realized about prolonging your grief is that your faith begins to wane, and without faith, no matter what you do or profess, it is impossible to please God. It is easy to trust in God when in certain times, but we learn to really trust Him in uncertain times.

Apostle Paul, throughout his epistles, encourages us to put away the old self and welcome the new. To inherit eternal life, we need to surrender all of our old ways, and put away completely the former self as we welcome the new. But we keep holding onto and mourning over our ashes, our old manner of self. We save a little of our old ways. We trust God, but not all the way, and we hold onto things of the past that we have no business carrying: old emotions that no longer serve us, like grief and certain relationships that we know are not good for us; old habits; beliefs that are outdated; painful events, and words that we fail to forgive; and all the while we wonder why we are not receiving the breakthrough or the miracle we so dearly need. I will tell you why. It is because of what you are holding onto. That is what is killing your future. For us to see beauty from our ashes, we need to surrender the old and welcome the new. Let go of what does not serve you. Pretending to be saved will not save you. Let go of the old and receive new life in Christ. Eternal life can only be found through surrendering yourself to God and letting Him take over your life completely, withholding nothing, not even treasured memories of people from your past. That is true surrender, abandoning yourself completely to the gracious love of God, and trusting that He will meet your every need.

What I realized about grief is that it opens you up to your new self, that is, if you let it transform you. It will reveal to you a strength inside yourself that you never knew existed. After grief comes another season, another valley, and another you.

Frederick Douglas, an American social activist, once said, "If there is no struggle, there is no progress." Your character is forged by the challenges you face and overcome. Your courage grows when you face your fears. Your strength and your faith are built as they are tested through your life experiences. We are all a little broken, but here is the beauty of it we can now put back the pieces in whatever way we want and make something new of ourselves.

Chapter 5: All things working together for my good

It is true that life, like a book, is best understood from the end to the beginning. I understood this while connecting the dots in my own life.

If someone had told me that losing both my parents would serve a greater purpose, I would have told them, there and then, that they were out of their mind. However, as I look back now, I realize that my parents died in time for me. The time was right for my growth; a growth that I would never have realized had I remained in their shade.

Soon after my mother's burial, I settled what was left of her estate, made sure my younger siblings were in boarding school, and then I went back to school. I had been away from university for almost two whole months and the school, obviously, had not closed because my mother had died. I had a lot of catching up to do, but thanks to my friends who always kept me informed on what was happening at school even in my absence, I was able to do so quickly.

My heart was still heavy with grief. I had just lost my mother, my life back home and everything that I was accustomed to. Sometimes when I was alone in my room, I would just break down and start crying. But even at my weakest and most vulnerable point, I still knew that God was in control.

Looking back over that whole period of my life, I realize that God had a much bigger plan for my life than I had ever envisioned. In essence, those difficult circumstances were exactly what I needed to shape and mold me for God's calling. I finally understood what it means to walk in faith. What, to me, seemed like a weakness, God used to become the wellspring of my strength. As apostle Paul writes in his letter to the Corinthians (2 Corinthians 1:3-4), Praise be to the God and Father of our Lord Jesus Christ, the father of compassion and the God of all comfort. Who comforts us in all our troubles, so that we can comfort those in any trouble with the same comfort we ourselves receive from God.

***

Back in university, my walk with God grew stronger as I had nothing to rely on but God's gracious love and mercy. My faith grew much stronger and bolder. Before my mother's death, I had pretty much been an on-and-off Christian. I had been mixing with different types of friends who would invite me to parties, and we would visit different places just to have fun. They were the typical college students that you see on TV and in the movies; they led carefree lives. When we would go to parties and stuff, I never really felt like I belonged. I always felt like an outsider looking in. Even though I was surrounded by people, I always felt a little different from them and at times, I would feel so lonely. After my mother's death, however, I found myself gravitating towards a different scene. On the nights that I used to go to a house party, I would go to a prayer meeting with other students on campus. I made friends at these prayer meetings, some of whom have, over the years, grown to be my unofficial family members.

We would meet in the girls' hostel and pray together. To avoid making noise for the other inhabitants of the hostel, we would find a secluded place and hold our prayer meetings there. Most times, we would hold our prayer meetings in the evenings, at midnight, as during this time, most people would be asleep. We would huddle together in a small kitchen in one of the hostels.

With time, people began to notice, and we would invite anyone interested. I witnessed a great movement of the Holy Spirit. Miracles happened, testimonies were shared, and souls were brought to the Lord. A lot of people started coming in and what started as a small group of people grew exponentially in number.

Other students on compass jokingly started calling us 'kitchen ministries', because we were always huddled in one kitchen or another, sharing the gospel and praying for each other.

Time seemed to move quickly, my final year in university passed by. Exam time came and people were busy preparing for their exams, especially the final year students, since these final exams would determine whether or not you got your degree.

We still met together for prayer groups and church services regularly, even during the usually stressful exam period. Surprisingly enough, our prayer group always seemed to grow in number during exam times. Mostly, it was because of some students who would be trying to pray for a last-minute miracle to save their grades and pass, despite their last-minute preparations.

***

The power of prayer

During one of our prayer meetings around this time, I remember one lady who came forward and asked to be prayed for because she was not feeling well. She had been to many places looking for help, in vain. We laid hands on her and prayed for her, and the woman came back a few days later with a testimony of how God had miraculously healed her. She did not feel any pain in her body. She could even do things she could not do before, and more. I understood then the power of prayer.

My prayer life began to grow stronger and stronger because I witnessed many miracles during the time I was in college. Through prayer, I was able to tap into the most mysterious stream of God's love flowing from within the depths of my heart.

Prayer has always been important to me. It has, in different moments in my life, been a source of comfort and strength. I believe communing with God and having a personal relationship with him is life changing.

God has called us to take a stand, and to be strong and courageous, in the face of life's many storms. We are called to obey God at whatever cost and to let success answer our critics. If it seems you have hit a hard place, or you've hit rock bottom in your personal life or ministry, don't wallow and complain. Don't keep thinking about it over and over, and offer reasons for it. Pray! Explanations and excuses rob us of strength and power. Don't spend your energy trying to avoid your problems. Use the authority that has been given you through Jesus and overthrow the demonic powers working against your life and gifting. Through prayer, take authority and make a clear path for the Spirit of God to minister into your life.

You need to train your spirit through prayer, and this in turn will produce invincible strength that will move whatever mountains that are in your way.

Over the years, I have met many people who struggle to have a consistent prayer life. I have been there too. But I realized that my struggles with praying consistently were because most times I was not engaging in a personal encounter with God. Prayer is essentially a personal encounter with God. For it to be a genuine and intimate encounter, you must come to God as you are. The real you. You must be ready to be truly yourself. Too often, truth is missing in our prayer because we do not show up as our real and honest selves, withholding nothing.

***

I wrote my final exams and returned home to Gweru to check on my siblings and see how they were doing. I had just started a small business of buying and selling different things; clothes, pots and anything that people ordered.

About a month later, my results came out and I had passed with a first-class degree. I was also one of the top students in my class. To say I was happy is an understatement. I could not believe that after everything

I had been through, I would be able to pass, let alone at the top of the class. I had passed the first hurdle, all by the grace of God.

About 2 months later, I graduated. My late mother's close friend (who we affectionately call Aunty Dapira), who has been like a mother to me, and a few of my friends and some of their family members came to the ceremony. It was definitely an occasion to celebrate. There were many tears of joy on the day. We enjoyed the celebration and festivities, basking in our success and thanking God for seeing us through. All those late nights of studying had finally paid off.

As I closed one chapter of my life, I was getting ready to begin yet another. After graduating, I did not waste any time. I immediately started applying for a job, and it was not easy. The first job I got was a teaching job in South Africa, at a high school in the Limpopo province. I taught economics to students in the 10th, 11th, and 12th grades. I remember being so grateful for the job because it had come at a time when I was struggling to get myself settled.

Less than a year after I started my teaching job, I was fortunate enough to find another that promised to be better than the first. I was called for an interview and I went. I had to ask for leave at the school so that I could go to my other job interview. I got to the place where the interview was taking place, participated in the interview, and was short listed. A few days later, I got a call and was told I got the job. But there was a catch: they wanted someone who had a car, and I did not have one at the time. It had been almost a year since I started working, but I had not saved up enough to buy a car. I had bought a few things for my new apartment and I would also send money to my younger siblings every other month. I had very little savings, and thank God there were no medical emergencies or a death in the family at the time, because that would have been catastrophic. Since I did not have a car, I could not celebrate the fact that I now had a better job. I, therefore, did the only thing I knew how to do; I prayed. I called a few of my friends and asked for prayers, but did not tell them what for, because I did not want to jinx the whole thing. I had been given only a few days before I started the new job. After praying for a miracle, I counted how much I had in my savings, and borrowed around from a few friends but after putting together everything I could gather, it still was not enough to cover the cost of a good, second-hand car. I needed this job desperately and I did not have plan B. So, about three days before I was due to report for work, I was busy checking car lots and online for a decent car I could afford with the few Rands I had. I had not quit my teaching job in case I could not get the new one because of my car issue.

While I was busy scouring for a car, I saw an advertisement of a car that I could afford. I did not even look at the pictures, I just asked if it could start and if it moved. I went to see the car and I was shocked. Well, considering I did not have enough money to buy a decent car, I could not complain much; but in all sincerity, I had expected more than what I saw. The guy at the car sale showed me this old rust bucket that looked like it belonged more in a museum than on the road. It was an old, creamish, Toyota Cressida, which I am pretty sure had its best days sometime in the early 90's. I haggled a bit and eventually bought it for a little less than the asking price. I planned to use it only for a few weeks or at least until I had enough money to buy a decent one.

I remember driving to my new job in this old car that had a surprisingly neat interior, with the engine making a loud ruckus. One of my managers asked me if the car was mine, and in my embarrassment, I told him it was my younger brother's, and mine was in the shop getting an engine problem fixed.

For the rest of the month, I used that car and drove it every day to and from work. It never had any problems, which, looking back, I think was nothing short of a miracle.

Later that month, after getting my first salary, I was determined to get a new car. I started looking for one immediately. Fortunately, after a few weeks, I found one, but I still could not afford it even if I were to sell my old car. I called my aunt (my mother's sister), and told her about the job and the money I needed for a new car. She agreed to loan me some money. I could finally afford a decent car. The next day, I went over to the car dealer's to buy the new car. I was over the moon. Things were finally going my way.

***

You and I cannot see, and at times cannot know what God has planned for us. That is why you should never believe that your worst fears are your fate or that when you are down, you will never rise again. You must have faith and courage to live your purpose boldly, and to pursue God's plan for your life. Then you must put all your fears and insecurities aside, and trust that you will find your way.

Chapter 6: Healed Wounds but ugly Scars

"Our wounds are often the openings into the best and most beautiful part of us."

-David Richo

In the opening of his book, the road less traveled, M. Scott Peck begins with the words: life is difficult, a statement which I very much concur with. Life presents us with many hardships and trials. Though we live through and survive these difficult times, moments and seasons in our lives, some painful memories endure and haunt us for lifetimes to come. It is only by the grace of God and through the power of His love that we can find healing and the power to transcend and transform through adversity. If or when we move forward, we usually come out stronger than we were before. I think the perversity of life is that in the struggle lies the joy and in overcoming our trials, we emerge stronger. It is often the case that the deep wells within our souls from which our joys arise are sometimes filled with our tears. Courage is often forged through pain, though not always. It is only when we acknowledge the pain and allow it to transform rather than ignoring or denying it. When we deny our pain, it grows, becomes fear or hate, and usually manifests as anger. Anger that is never transformed becomes resentment and bitterness, and bitterness is not good for the soul.

***

Generational wounds

They say a girl's first love is her father, but I did not have much of a relationship with my father. During the years when my parents' relationship was struggling, I began, little by little, to resent my father. This was because of the abuse we suffered at his hands. It took me many years to acknowledge the hurt, the pain and the anger, and it took me even longer to heal and find my way back to wholeness (I am not all the way there yet, but thanks be to God, I am not where I used to be).

There is a saying that goes: when you don't know what to do, you do what you know. My parents both grew up in abusive homes. They grew up in an environment with traditional masculine figures who perpetuated an image of toxic masculinity, an environment that encouraged the disciplining of women and children through violence, where fear was mistaken for respect. And when the time came for my father to have his own family, he did what he knew, with the tools he had at the time.

Looking back, I realize my father was a lost man. He did not really fit in. On the surface, he seemed to be fine but I suspect that deep down, there was a lot of pain, anger and bitterness that haunted him. It always seemed to me that his outward persona was inauthentic. He seemed like he was hiding something from everyone, and mostly from himself. It was the pain of his past that he was trying to hide, but because these old wounds from his past never saw the light of day, they never healed. I always felt it was this that made him seem so lonely, and it was this loneliness that drove him into a life-long search. He searched relentlessly in bottles, under women's skirts, and in lofty job titles for himself; lost in a distant time, lost to himself and everyone else, and he was never found since. It was obvious to me then that he had never belonged in any place, and that sense of not belonging left him searching for his self in places he never was.

Because my father's wounds never healed (and his father's before him), those generational wounds and pain began to manifest in my life. Generational pain is difficult to heal from, and is often well disguised in the temples of our souls to the extent that we never realize its existence, though its fruits are apparent in our thoughts, words and deeds.

Pain was a gift I often gave without intention, because it is the only thing I had allowed myself to feel for a long time. I was bitter, and that root of bitterness was slowly starting to contaminate my soul.

There is a saying that goes: time heals all wounds. It has gained popularity over the years, and I believe such thinking is at the root of many people's unresolved pain and trauma. Time passing, by itself, does not do much, except perhaps help us forget a little. But forgetting and healing are not the same thing. It is all the things that we do that help us to heal and break the cycles of generational pain, that help us to heal and move on. For those of us that accept the ideology of the passage of time and resist making any changes, we should not expect to see much difference in our lives.

If you carry all the emotional hurt and pain of your past and do nothing to address the trauma within you, sure, overtime, you might not think about it as much, but it will never be too far from the surface. Those emotional wounds will be ready to rip right open again at the slightest suggestion of any kind of trouble.

Because of the relationship I had with my father, I never really trusted men in general. As a result, I could never have a deep, intimate and lasting relationship. Without trust, it is difficult and almost impossible to build any kind of relationship or have meaningful connections with other people.

***

Unequally yoked

Sometimes, when you think the worst is behind you, just as life appears to be finally going your way and things seem to be flowing, a huge speed bump arises directly in your path and everything turns upside down. The next thing you know is you are picking up broken pieces of your life, trying to piece it back together, not knowing if it will ever be same again. Have you ever had those moments? I have and, trust me, it is never a good feeling.

Not long after I started my second job, I met Brandon, the man who later became my fiancé (now ex-fiancé). He was quite handsome and charming at first. It was the beginning of my very own happy-ever-after fairytale, or so I thought. We connected and started seeing more and more of each other. It was easy to open up to him. He was patient with me, granted at the time I was not easy to be around because I was a bitter person and still dealing with the pain from my past. Slowly, we got to know each other. I shared my life story with him and he did the same. We both came from troubled families, haunted by domestic violence. Because we had a similar past, we bonded over our traumas. Little did I know that there is a clear difference between trauma-bonding and love. At the time, I did not know how to tell the difference or even if there was a difference at all.

I was in love, or so I thought, and that was all that mattered to me.

My relationship with my ex had a harmonious beginning. There was, at first, an undeniable pull that drew us together, but there was also a distance between us created by our unhealed hearts. This space within us and between us, filled with the unseen and unknown traumas from our past, caused miscommunication, friction and sometimes even unintentional pain. It is difficult to build an intimate relationship with someone when you are still a mystery to yourself. It can only occur when both partners commit to turning inward, to heal/ know yourselves. Naturally, this brings you closer together and it elevates the love and support you give each other.

When you are dating a narcissist, it is usually difficult to tell from the onset. It is only in retrospect that you can see the manipulation and the gas lighting and call it what it is, but when you build a relationship on a foundation of lies, the truth will break it apart. I remember the earlier fights my ex and I used to have. He would hit me and then later apologize for losing his temper and promise that it would not happen again. It happened, again and again. It was a clear red flag I should have seen, but I was so determined to make my relationship work. I was always quick to fade his flaws, even when my family members would criticize him. I did not clearly see the all-too-familiar pattern. I was so worried about what people would say if my engagement and relationship collapsed within such a short space of time, so I bit the bullet, so to speak, and got stuck in a relationship which I knew was not healthy. I got encouraged by some friends and pastors, and I kept holding on. Little did I know that I was making the most common and the most painful mistake women have made all throughout the ages: to naively think that with their love, they can change the men they love. In retrospect, I realize that sometimes I was so busy praying and telling God what I wanted in my life, that I could not hear Him telling me, instead, what I needed. My will was not totally surrendered to His will. Only when we have surrendered our will to His will can we see and know what His perfect will for our lives is.

A few months after we got engaged, my ex-fiancé convinced me to quit my job and start working for his startup company. Given my past experience working in different administrative roles, I thought it would be a good idea, and I thought maybe working as a team would also be healthy for our relationship. We agreed that I would handle the day-to-day management while he handled the operational side of the business. Little did I know that he planned to take away my earning power so I would be dependent on him financially. I did not think of it that way at the time. I just thought it was a good idea, for us to focus on our little startup and grow it.

We started disagreeing over how to run the business, and it was not just normal couples disagreeing over conflicting values. Most of our disagreements would escalate into fistfights. All this was familiar to me, and it seemed as if my parents' relationship was repeating itself. It was a cycle that needed to be broken.

It is true what the old age maxim says - hurt people hurt people. Brandon and I were both broken people and we were trying to build a relationship and marriage with the splintered pieces from our broken pasts. We were not well equipped to deal with our relationship problems because we had not taken time to heal from the trauma and abuse we had endured at the hands of our primary caregivers.

My fiancés' startup business started struggling. Most of his clients started using and preferring larger and established companies. I had to find a job, I thought and started applying for one, unknown to my fiancé. After a few attempts, I found a new job. I told Brandon and though he was reluctant at first, l convinced him that it would help us in the short term and once things were more stable at the company, I would return.

I found a job in a small town outside of Johannesburg. At the time however, l was about two months pregnant. I had not told this to my new employer. When my pregnancy was about three months old, it started showing. My new bosses were unhappy about this and they called me for a disciplinary meeting in Johannesburg. They sent me an email to that effect, but the email was not clear what the issue to be discussed was about. Before the date of the meeting, I hiked to Midrand where l was staying at the time with my fiance. It was a few minutes' walk from the company headquarters where the meeting would take place the next day.

The next morning, l went to the company headquarters where l met with the human resources manager (HRM) and two company lawyers. The HRM explained to me the purpose of the meeting, which was the termination of my contract because l had been deceitful in my job application. They argued that l had not been honest with them, and I had not told them beforehand about my pregnancy, and they said that was cause for termination. I was angry and shocked. I tried to explain to them that it was something that I had also just found out. Furthermore, it was not a basis to discriminate against me from getting the job.

The lawyers gave me a piece of paper to sign, that stated that I was agreeing to my termination. I signed the paper and left. I told my close friends about the matter and they told me to take the company to labor court for unlawful termination. I, however, insisted against it. I had just been fired, and I wanted to put the whole thing behind me. I kept praying about it and asked why me God, but no answer came. I realized that sometimes, the answers we seek from God are not readily available, but this does not mean they are not there. Faith requires that we sometimes have to wait for God to reveal his plan for us. Sometimes, when we ask questions and seek answers, we come to one conclusion, that is, God's vision for our lives is much greater than our own.

***

After I lost the job, I decided to move on. I believe that when God closes a door or lets it close, it is always for a good reason, and though we cannot see it at the time, it is always for our growth.

I kept looking for jobs, in hope more than realistic expectation. This was because my pregnancy was getting heavier and I did not think anyone would hire a heavily pregnant woman, but I still tried.

The situation at home with my fiancé had not mellowed. He and I still fought, and it seemed the more we stayed together, the better we got at it. Our house started to feel like a war zone and every conversation we had felt like it was riddled with land mines. One wrong word could cause an explosion. There would be moments of peace in our house, but they were short-lived.

When I was about 7 months pregnant, I was under so much stress because of the toxic home environment. I remember my ankles would swell, as well as my wrists. It was around this time that I started having these unbearable stomach cramps. I was in so much pain. I woke my fiancé up in the middle of the night and asked him to take me to hospital. When we arrived, I was attended to by the doctor on duty that evening. They did a few tests and afterwards told me to rest for a while, whilst they ran some tests. A few minutes later, another doctor came in with the one who had examined me earlier. He asked me a few questions, which I answered whilst he did a physical exam. Afterward, the doctor told me that I was in labor and they had to schedule an emergency C-section. "How could this be?" I asked. They told me that it was not uncommon for such things to happen. The doctors explained that it usually happens when the mother is under a lot of stress. They assured me they would do their best to ensure a safe delivery.

Brandon was in more shock than I was. He rushed home to get a few clothes and supplies that I might need.

I was prepped for theater, and as I was being wheeled to the operating room, I kept praying for a safe delivery. A few hours later, I woke up in a haze and was told I had given birth to a baby boy. The nurse told me that he was doing okay and once I had regained my strength and the drugs had worn off, she would take me to see him.

A little later, after the anesthetic had worn off, one of the nurses on duty took me to see my baby. I walked into this room with babies in incubators, and I was shown this tiny human being. He was so small I could lift him with one hand; this little human being holding on to dear life. There were so many tubes and needles on him. I was so close to tears and wanted to cry, but the nurse who was with me told me not to cry because the worst was already behind us.

A few minutes later, my fiancé came. We went and saw our child together. We had decided that if our first child was a boy, we would name him Israel. As we saw Israel, we met one of the doctors who had performed the emergency C-section. He told us that Israel had been born with under-developed lungs and so he could not breathe on his own. They put him on life support machines while injecting him with growth hormones to help speed up his lung growth. My friends and family came offering words of comfort and strength, and our church pastor at the time came and we prayed for Israel together.

A few days later, the doctors told us that they were monitoring Israel's situation and very little had changed. They told us his lung development was too slow and that his chances of survival were slim, and if they removed the life support system, he was unlikely to survive. I was distraught. God had given me hope when I conceived a son, and now I felt like all that hope was being taken away. I prayed that something might change, but nothing did. I felt so alone and so isolated. I felt as though God had abandoned me. It is one thing to lose a parent, but nothing in the world felt worse than the possibility of losing a child.

I was mourning even when little Israel was still fighting for dear life. My pastor came and told me to have faith in the miracle working power of God, but to me it seemed we were hoping against hope. The pastor kept telling me that God is on our side and all I needed was to be strong and courageous.

A few days later, Israel passed on. I was heartbroken, to say the least, and just writing about this takes me back to those painful moments of my past. Nothing can prepare you for the death of a loved one, especially the death of a child. It changes you.

The death of Israel brought with it much pain and sadness in my life, and strangely enough, it also brought clarity into my life. It was as if a veil had lifted and I could see things that I could not before. For the first time since I got engaged with Brandon, I could finally admit to myself that we did not have a healthy relationship. I had struggled with the thought in my mind for a while. Earlier, I had thought it would change, but I realized that I had no power to change anybody else but me. I decided, in that moment, to leave the relationship.

To break a cycle, you need, firstly, to acknowledge it and begin to do your inner work. You need to learn to own your triggers and learn to manage your emotions. Because I had not healed from the pain and anger I carried from my past relationship with my father, I ended up marrying someone just like my father.

God leads us through different seasons in our lives so that we learn the lessons he wants to teach. Whenever we do not learn the lesson or pass the test, the lesson is bound to repeat itself until we learn it. He might change the classroom and even the teachers, but the lesson is still the same.

***

Healing old wounds

The thing about wounds though is that, even though they heal, some leave ugly scars. I imagine deep traumas and painful memories are like wounds to our souls, wounds that, if we do not take time to acknowledge and heal, can end up infecting our whole being.

As a child, I enjoyed reading bible stories a lot, but I never really understood one story in particular, that of Ananias and Sapphira. It always made me feel unsettled. I always thought to myself, how can a gracious and merciful God punish people who sold their land and possessions, literally all they had, to give to the poor? Reading the text now, I realized that there is more to it than people being struck down dead for lying about keeping some of the proceeds from the sale of their property. As the church, we are called to eternal life in and through Christ Jesus. Apostle Paul, throughout his epistles, encourages us to put away the old self and welcome the new. To inherit eternal life, we need to surrender all of our old ways, and put away completely the former self as we welcome the new, but we keep holding onto our old manner of self. We save a little of our old ways. We trust God, but not all the way, and we hold onto things of the past that we have no business carrying: old emotions that no longer serve us, like grief and certain relationships that we know are not good for us; old habits; beliefs that are outdated; painful events, and words that we fail to forgive; and all the while, we wonder why we are not receiving the breakthrough or the miracle we so dearly need. I will tell you why. It is because of what you are holding onto. That is what is killing your future. So, surrender the old and welcome the new. Let go of what does not serve you. Pretending to be saved will not save you. Let go of the old and receive new life in Christ. Eternal life can only be found through surrendering yourself to God and letting Him take over your life completely, withholding nothing. That is true surrender, abandoning yourself completely to the gracious love of God, and trusting that He will meet your every need.

Chapter 7: Faith in Action

I've met many people who reach out to me, and ask for prayers and advice concerning challenges they are facing. Often, these people know what they need to do but they struggle with fear and self-doubt. They are afraid of taking the first step and trusting that God will see them through. I too, have felt the same way. I have felt stuck in places and situations I know too well I do not belong in. Fear and anxiety about the future kept me captive for a while, until I finally made the decision to act on faith. I made the decision to step out of my self-made prison, and to step into the life God called me to live.

I have discovered time and again that when we ask God's help and then take action, knowing in our hearts that He is watching over us, there is no reason to be fearful.

***

A few months after the untimely death of my first child, I discovered that I was pregnant again. I was filled with mixed emotions at first, but I put my faith into action. I surrendered everything into God's hands. During that time, my fiancé was struggling to find work to do, and the situation at home became more toxic. I kept praying that God would open new doors for his business, and that he would also change his heart. It, however, seemed as if things were slowly becoming worse.

Nine anxious and prayer filled months later, I gave birth to a beautiful bouncing baby girl. She was named Atarah by her father. Those who know me (and know Atarah) know what a blessing she is to me and to the rest of our family. She is my bundle of Joy.

Children are surely special gifts from God. It is a blessing to be a steward and to care for them. Parenting is one job that you start with little to no training at all; it is one job that you are given even if you have limited to no experience at all. It will humble you many times, and it transforms you, in a big way.

When Atarah was about 7 months old, I decided to start working again, since we were struggling financially and my husband's business was not doing so well. I started applying for jobs. I thought maybe if I worked, we would have enough to go by financially, and it would ease the tension in our home. After a few months of searching, in January of 2018, I found a job. However, there were conditions. I was given the job on the condition that I go on a 3-month probationary period to do the required training and to see if I could do the job well. I had decided to look for a babysitter who would take care of my baby while I was away at work.

After I started work, my fiancé started acting strangely. At times, he would not come home and he would offer little to no explanation. It did not bother me at first since I was so busy trying to impress my new bosses. I would be busy reading operations manuals at night. This happened for a time, until one day he packed his things and left. For good. I was exhausted physically from my job and emotionally drained by the relationship itself so much that I did not even know how to react. I had reached my breaking point and the on-and-off of our relationship had taken its toll. The one thing that kept me going at the time was my daughter. I was determined to go through thick and thin to make sure she had food to eat, clothes on her back and a warm bed to sleep in. She would have everything I could give and I would make sure of it.

Here I was with a small child, a meagre salary and no fiance. I was going through all this and yet somehow, I was at peace. I just knew that one way or another, I was going to make it through. I knew God would make a way for me. That is the power of faith. It gives you hope in an otherwise hopeless situation. I did not even tell my family what was going on, not because they are not supportive; in fact, my immediate family is quite supportive. Whenever one of us has a problem, we huddle together and help each other out. You could call them up at any time of the day and they will be there to help. There are many times I have turned to my family for love and support and they have been pillars of strength for me. But as I was going through this period of putting my faith in action, I started witnessing the mountain-moving power of God at work in my life.

Having faith, beliefs and conviction is a great thing, but your life is measured by the actions you take based upon your beliefs.

In three months, I finished my probation period at my new job. They decided I was good enough and they hired me full-time. I was given a full salary, allowances and the use of a company car. I could now afford to rent a new apartment for myself, my daughter and our new live-in nanny.

When God begins to work miracles in your life and doors that were once closed begin to open, you can easily forget the pain of your past struggles. If you wait upon the lord and trust in him, you will find renewed strength. But waiting on God does not mean you sit by the sidelines and watch while life is passing you by. It does not mean you stop living your life in case something bad happens or things spiral out of control. It means, however, that in whatever you find to do, you always do your best and let God do the rest. It means you put your faith in action and take whatever opportunity is given to you, trusting that God will see you through.

There are times though, when I struggle to recover from a setback. A major crisis like losing a job, a financial problem, a broken relationship, or the loss of a loved one can be difficult for anyone to manage. During such times, even a relatively minor challenge can seem insurmountable if you are already struggling. If you find yourself struggling, as I have, my recommended recovery plan is to lean, with gratitude, on those who care about you. Be patient with your tender feelings, do your best to understand the realities versus the emotions at play, and put your faith into action. As hard as it may seem, move forward one step at a time, day by day, knowing that there will be valuable lessons learned and strength gained in each trial. There is a certain peace to be found in knowing that there is a master plan for your life, and that your value, purpose and destiny are not determined by what happens to you, but by how you respond.

***

The power of letting go

When the Lamb of God, Jesus Christ, was slain, and died for our sins on the cross, his last words were "It is finished!" Those words were not just a prophecy of his impending death, but a triumphant declaration of victory. He conquered the power of sin and reigned victorious over the world and all principalities therein. Through Him and in Him, we too reign victoriously! We are victors not victims. When he said 'It is finished', he meant the chains of slavery to sin had been broken. No longer are we to live in fear, but in fullness of love. No longer are we bound by the law, but we are clothed by a cloak of grace. Thus, continue to declare and prophecy that 'it is finished' to your failures, to your struggles, to your sickness, to your disappointments, to your poverty, to your lack of progress in life, and to whatever problem you might face or are facing in your life.

When God wants to do something in your life, there is always a shift that takes place. There is always a change in the environment (spiritual, physical, or emotional). He will lead you outside of your comfort zone into unfamiliar territory, which I like to call the wilderness. It is in this wilderness that your faith grows, as you learn to rely more on him than on your own strength.

***

Trusting the process

Every single day, God reveals his plan for me. Over the years, I have learnt to trust the process because it is in the process that God molds and perfects us.

Trusting the process is an act of courage. It takes courage to surrender everything into God's hands, and to have full assurance that no matter what happens, God's plan will prevail.

When I began to trust the process, I started to focus more on solutions rather than on problems. I focused more on doing than on wallowing in self-pity. I found I had more clarity even in uncertain times. I began to trust myself more because I understood and believed that I was gifted by God and made for a purpose. In the year I started my new job at KFC, new doors began to open for me. It was a season of breakthrough in my life.

.... Sometimes we claim that we are waiting on God, but in actuality God is waiting on us. He is waiting for us to grow and to cultivate our inner strength.

During my weekends, I started taking baking classes. It was a hobby at first. I started baking cakes and selling them, and to my surprise, I got great reviews from everyone. I then decided to start a company, my very own bakery. I named my small baking business, Sweet encounter. Since I was just starting out and testing the waters, I did not need much space at all. I could do everything while I was at home. I starting baking cakes and small pastries for people who ordered them for various functions.

Chapter 8: the power oF purpose

"The two most important days in your life are the day you are born and the day you understand why"
- Mark Twain
"Don't deny the world of the blessing that you are"
- Tinashe Mujera

When you accept, with faith, that you will find your purpose, and then move step by step on the path to discovery, you will find, as I have, that God's vision for your life is far greater than anything you might imagine. This does not mean that your every wish will be granted and that all your dreams will come true, but what I realized and also continue to witness is that no part of your life experience is a waste. Everything happens for a reason. Though I do not receive every miracle I pray for, I have seen many times that I can be a miracle to someone else. I can be a miracle that opens your eyes, inspires you, instills courage in the heart, assures you that you are loved, and sends you forward to serve your purpose.

***

One of my all-time favorite quotes by David Viscott is 'The purpose of life is to discover your gift. The work of life is to develop it. The meaning of life is to give your gift away'. It taught me early that the meaning of life is intricately woven with purpose, and that there is no gifting without purpose, and no purpose without serving.

Growing up, I enjoyed watching superhero movies. There is always that moment in the movie when the hero discovers his or her superpower, and then that character defining moment when they use their super power to serve others. I have always imagined our lives are quite similar to that. When you discover what makes you uniquely you, and apply it to the life you envision - you become, at that moment, your own life's hero.

I found God's purpose for me over time and I realized that I am, indeed, a child of God who was made for a reason. Though I cannot say I know everything God has in store for me, I am confident that whatever the reason, it is well.

Winston Churchill once said, "You make a living by what you get. You make a life by what you give." Whenever I ask people about the most fulfilling aspects of their lives, they always talk about sharing with others. The true nature of human beings isn't selfish. Our life purpose and meaning is always found in and through serving others.

It is one thing to know what your life purpose is, and another to step out and begin to live it out. Some people know what their life purpose is but they are not actively living it out. Sometimes we pursue one goal or another, and yet these goals are not aligned to any of our life values. Even if we achieve these said goals, we never find fulfillment, because we are not consistent with our meta goals, our core beliefs. This is perhaps one of the greatest causes of our frustration, anxiety, stress, and mental health issues. It is important to make the distinction between achieving your goals and living out your values.

When you want to live with purpose, you have to discover your life values and learn to live in alignment with them. When you know what your life values are and live consistently, you will feel energized, connected, and stimulated, and when you do what you love, you will do more than succeed: you will soar.

Now, each one of us has a different set of values. As I said earlier, it is important to know what your values are and list them in order of priority. This is essential because sometimes, we have value conflicts, and knowing your priorities will help you in your decision making. When you pick what is more important to you, you will always find fulfillment.

Stepping into your God-given calling is the greatest thing you can do for yourself and others. There is no greater gift you can give or receive than to honor your calling. It is why you were born and how you become most truly alive. When you understand your purpose and begin to live it out, you have found your power. Pay attention to what feeds your energy, because there is no real doing without first being.

Reading the story of Jesus feeding the five thousand, I always wondered at what point the bread multiplied. After a while, I realized that the miracle was in the breaking. As he broke the bread into pieces, it multiplied. This got me thinking about my own life. Our instinct is always to self-preserve. We stick to what is comfortable, to the known predictable way. We are afraid to break. We are afraid of facing new challenges and adversities that come our way. That is why, I believe, we are not growing or seeing miracles happening in our daily lives. The miracle always happens when you readily face the challenges in your own life. It happens when you have reached the end of your own strength and you believe there is nothing left to give. We all have different 'breaking points'. For David, it was when he faced Goliath; for Peter, it was when he stepped out of the boat and walked on water as on dry ground; for Job, it was when he lost everything he had. If there is any takeaway from those stories, it is, 'don't be afraid to face challenges that come your way. Do not be afraid to break'. It is always when you are 'broken' where you have the most to give. These are the scars of your purpose. I tell you this now, whatever challenges you might be facing, they are there to break you, and they are there to grow you. Recently, I was working in my orchard and I was observing this mango tree. It had not been fruitful for the past 2 years but last year, I decided to prune it a little bit, and guess what?!! It became fruitful! Challenges and adversity will prune you, but do not be afraid, it is so you can bear fruit. It is in the breaking that you will see miracles begin to happen.

***

The power of love

Living a purpose-driven life comes down to love: When you care enough for others to serve them, to help them, to inspire them and to encourage them. It always comes back to love. We have a power to love without limits and we need to activate that love, not just to fulfill our purpose, but to play a part in seeing the whole world come to peace and fulfillment. Apostle Paul writes, "If I speak in the tongues of men or of angels, but do not have love, I am only a resounding cymbal. If I have faith that can

move mountains but do not have love, I am nothing."

In a world that seems callous and cruel, we tend to lose sight of the fact that God loves us so much He sent His Son to pay the price and die for us. He is always there for us. When you know and have experienced the love of God, all you want to do is love Him and everyone around you. You may forget that sometimes, I know at one point in my life I have. Yet, I have found that when I am most confused about God's plan for me, when I am seriously struggling to figure out what I should do to serve His purpose, He will place someone in my path or create a situation to reveal that purpose or to test whether I walk the talk. To my surprise, the business grew in such a short space of time. I started to get more orders than I could meet in one weekend. I was filled with so much gratitude. Because I was getting so many orders, I started asking my sister to help me.

If you have faith, you do not need proof; you live it. You do not even need to have all the right answers, all you need are the right questions. No one knows what the future holds. Most of the time, God's plan is beyond our grasp and often even beyond our imaginations!

Acknowledgements

As I look back on the many transformational moments in my life, I see the faces of so many extraordinary human beings.

Briefly here, I'd like to express my deep gratitude to those who have touched my life and brought me back on course from time to time to make this book a reality.

Firstly, I'd like to thank my family. Thank you for your love and support through thick and thin, I love you. To my mentors, in particular Elder Isaiah-Phillips Akintola, I'm forever grateful for your advice, insight, perspective, prayers, encouragement, strategies, love, and care. You are the shoulders I stand on.

To my friends, colleagues and sisters that became family thank you for going on this journey with me. It's been a blessing. To my editor Rebecca who made my writing even better and to the team at Boutique books for making this publication a success.

Special thanks to Diron and the team at Mark on Africa Digital, for the beautiful cover design. To my sister Ncumisa, for the beautiful cover picture.

Nashe -With God- The journey of a Transformed woman

Don't miss out!

Visit the website below and you can sign up to receive emails whenever Tinashe Mujera publishes a new book. There's no charge and no obligation.

https://books2read.com/r/B-A-GPCHB-IZHBD

BOOKS 2 READ

Connecting independent readers to independent writers.

About the Author

Tinashe Mujera, well-known as Coach Tina, is a life skills coach and a beacon of transformation and empowerment. As the author of "NASHE - WITH GOD – The Journey of a Transformed Woman," she shares her remarkable story of personal growth and spiritual awakening.

Born into adversity, Coach Tina faced numerous challenges on her journey to self-discovery. However, through unwavering faith and determination, she navigated the trials of life with grace and resilience.

A passionate advocate for positive change, Coach Tina has dedicated her life to inspiring others to reach their full potential. As a coach and mentor, she empowers individuals to overcome obstacles, embrace their true selves, and live authentically.

"NASHE - WITH GOD" chronicles Coach Tina's transformative journey, offering insights, wisdom, and guidance for those seeking inner peace and fulfillment. Through her story, readers are encouraged to cultivate faith, resilience, and a deep connection with the divine.

Tinashe Mujera, widely recognized as Coach Tina, delivers a profound message of hope and spiritual awakening, igniting a powerful movement of personal transformation and healing worldwide.

Read more at https://coachtina.co.za/.